ST. RAGE'S VAULT

ST. RAGE'S VAULT

B. K. Fischer

WINNER OF THE 2012 WASHINGTON PRIZE

THE WORD WORKS
WASHINGTON, D.C.

FIRST EDITION, FIRST PRINTING
St. Rage's Vault
Copyright © 2013 by B.K. Fischer

Reproduction of any part of this book in any form or by any means, electronic or mechanical, except when quoted in part for the purpose of review, must be with permission from the publisher in writing. Address inquiries to:

The WORD WORKS
PO Box 42164
Washington, DC 20015

wordworksbooks.org
editor@wordworksbooks.org

Cover art: "Nude in Red," (2010, oil on linen)
  by Sarah Griffin Thibodeaux
  www.sarahgriffinthibodeaux.com

Author's photo: Dan Fried

Book design, typography: Janice Olson

Library of Congress Control Number: 2012950824
International Standard Book Number: 978-0-915380-84-8

ACKNOWLEDGMENTS

Grateful acknowledgment to the editors of the journals where versions of these poems first appeared:

Boston Review, "Arachne: Recent Memory"
Crab Orchard Review, "Highchair," "Maternity Bathing Suit"
Ekphrasis, "Nocturne," as "Luminous Zag: Night"
FIELD, "Blue Nudes," "Interruption," as "Interruption by Archangel"
The Hopkins Review, "Willow Grove, Pennsylvania, 1931"
LEVELER, "Week 36 (Figure)"
Literary Mama, "Fabrication"
The Paris Review, "Thought," as "Jane in the Box"
Southwest Review, "Suburban Chagall"
Western Humanities Review, "St. Rage's Vault"
WSQ, "Wired," as "Electric Dress"

"Mothership" was produced as a play on January 24 and 27, 2008, as part of *Image & Script*, Hudson Valley Center for Contemporary Art, Peekskill, New York, with Teri Anzalone, directed by Mara Mills.

Gratitudes for this book go back a long way. For the gifts of attention, discernment, and cheer I received while writing these poems and gathering them together, I owe countless thanks. To Richard Howard, Mary Jo Bang, Timothy Donnelly, Stephanie Strickland, and the late Kenneth Koch. To Karren Alenier, Nancy White, and Janice Olson at The Word Works. To Erin Donovan, Troy Thibodeaux, Sarah Thibodeaux, Heather Hewett, Jennifer Franklin, Bill Waddell, and Jo Ann Clark.

To Kathryn Fischer, Dottie Pfohl, Gina Vercesi, Kristin Wuerffel, Margaret Yawman, Louise O'Sullivan, Amy Poret, Jennifer Green, Michelle Stratman, Nicole Valente, Amanda and Spencer Kozinn, Peter and Alison Fischer, and all the Allendorfs—for esprit de corps and heavy lifting on the homefront. To my parents, Peter and Donna Fischer, for giving me the courage to bring children into the world in the first place. To my grandfather, Joseph Cassidy. To John—flames begotten of flame.

for James, Emily, & Lauren

CONTENTS

I.

WEEK 1	(Interruption)	13
WEEK 2	(Thought)	14
WEEK 3	(Arachne: Recent Memory)	15
WEEK 4	(Fabrication)	17
WEEK 5	(Figure)	18
WEEK 6	(Landscape with Baby and Dog)	19
WEEK 7	(Figure)	20
WEEK 8	(Organogenesis)	21
WEEK 9	(Fear)	22
WEEK 10	(Figure)	23
WEEK 11	(Trade Routes)	24
WEEK 12	(Figure)	25
WEEK 13	(Blue Reading)	26

II.

WEEK 14	(Suburban Chagall)	31
WEEK 15	(Quickening)	32
WEEK 16	(Highchair)	33
WEEK 17	(Three Girls)	34
WEEK 18	(Word of Mouth)	35
WEEK 19	(White Vertical Water)	37
WEEK 20	(Middle Distance)	39
WEEK 21	(Still Life)	40
WEEK 22	(Anacoluthon)	42

WEEK 23 (Exposure)	44
WEEK 24 (Viability)	46
WEEK 25 (Biopsy)	48
WEEK 26 (St. Rage's Vault)	49

III.

WEEK 27 (Figure)	55
WEEK 28 (Stone Child)	56
WEEK 29 (Goodnight Nobody)	58
WEEK 30 (Maternity Bathing Suit)	59
WEEK 31 (Chaos Blame Trust)	60
WEEK 32 (Willow Grove, Pennsylvania, 1931)	61
WEEK 33 (Weaning the Christ)	62
WEEK 34 (Wired)	63
WEEK 35 (Mothership)	64
WEEK 36 (Figure)	68
WEEK 37 (Tachycardia)	69
WEEK 38 (Figure)	71
WEEK 39 (Blue Nudes)	72
WEEK 40 (Nocturne)	74
NOTES	76
About the Author /About the Artist	80
About the Washington Prize	81
About The Word Works	82

I.

Week 1 (Interruption)

The angel is adamant,
rat-face mean—*up yours*
says the finger and so it happens,
the whole run of luck
from the almost-stoning to the stone.

Can't you see she's trying to read?
She keeps her thumb in the book,
thinking she'll get back to it,

but there's a smudge on the edge
of the elongated outline, a fuss
where the doves were erased
except for their crossed tails,

a cornice of sorts that crowns
the usual portals with six or seven
inscrutable characters.

He clears his throat. She
clutches her collar shut, as if
that would do any good.
That alleged yes.

Week 2 (Thought)

Undone, she's only a head, a fine
cheek and throat his chisel cut.
She waits to become a thought,
rough-cornered, rests her chin

on the block. Her bonnet anchors
the curve his firm hand folded
from stone to hold her pate solid.
No trunk or limbs, the cube blanks

her eyes, full-brimmed, unreleased,
but its weight bears down, bears up
its shapes—shoulder, lovelock. Deep
in white, she flinches, draws her knees

near to unhinging. She remembers
her body, the way it went unwatched.
He promised nothing tragic could
ever come of poses, reveries,

and she consented to composure.
She set her jaw, and haughtiness
restrained her, chilled her hands—
her body not a body but an ore.

Stones are patient clothes. Days
on days she learns his craft, his process,
with one fixed eye—Adonis across
the room in his muscular bronzes,

the goddess over him: she likes
the way he lies and takes the kiss
so still, until she sees he is
left for dead. I am, she thinks,

the right girl: good, dumbstruck.

WEEK 3 (Arachne: Recent Memory)

I amuse myself with bits
    of cellophane, fluff caught
in the weave with the clipart—guitar
    strung on the shell of an armadillo,
graphics from Tuesday's forecast.
    I've run out of images, used up the erotic
exploits of the gods. Anatomy limits
    the possibilities for penetration
and thread is not dear.
    A slow week: a piece on pangs
of drowning in black and white, the latest
    alien abduction narrative—
though cool space speculums don't come
    across on cloth—a sketch of men astride
inspired by a horse race in Dubai,
    some footstool embroidery
for William Satan, a birthday whim
    at the suggestion of mutual friends.
It's easy to succumb to stasis, savage
    inaction, shuttle dropped to the floor,
my favorite cagey dodge about
    a hole in aboutness when it's all
about the loom, defunct.

    Toy a bit with Billy—I must admit
I like his type, shaving-cream daddy
    who'll pick me up, put
my lips to his taut cheekbone. I miss
    the odd balance of a body
on another body stretched and resting,
    like sleeping on a slight incline
you didn't sense when you pitched the tent.
    Bipeds have it good.

All the talk about erotics of the visual,
        but gaze all you like,
this patchwork dalliance remains
        inscrutable—yesterday's scene of legs
over shoulders, diaper-change style.
        The last time the tapestry of ravish
actually got seen was when
        the women saw the Resurrection,
the tanned ankles of Jesus,
        wept on and ringed in their grips,
Jesus on the road to the Emmys, strolling
        between sex and the thought of sex.

There's still the fans, the fantasy
        of a fair share of art in punishment.
Mail from one Wanda who suggests
        the buffeted souls in lust are served
buffet-style with hunks of parmagiana.
        Snapshot of the track star
from Mineola Prep who arrives
        at last at the Arctic Circle,
strips, and pumps the air. A woman
        in Kissimmee says she killed
a giant spider behind her toilet bowl
        only to watch in horror while its body
released a thousand offspring,
        bitties that poured to the corners
while the mama shriveled small.
        I weave them in for lack
of better options, tangents, fields of play
        to take my mind off the rasp
that sounds, soulless and dry,
        when I strum my legs together like a lyre.

Week 4 (Fabrication)

We made her the usual way,
with spools and cocoons and a wisp
of frayed thread. That business

about the woof took time.
We spun her up and wondered

whose side is she on, anyway?
Whose eyes and the slouch
of whose shoulders? We loomed

over her day and night, sometimes
offering the wrong thing.

We gave her a name,
a counterpane and a slap,
sang songs about a larva

that were both kind and true.
She wriggled right out

of the swaddling as soon as
we got the story going.

Week 5 (Figure)

Squeezed in that sack of a dress,
she's segmented—head, thorax,
abdomen—spilling out of her

undergarments in spite of herself,
showing the swell in hip and jowl,
pout and poof and massive brow,

hair everywhere—in her eyes,
in the shadows, a grab of it
gripped in elastic, eyes gashed

with the same black that steadies
the shoulders, her back to the plaster:
a shabby room, tally marks scored

in the wallboard—countdown,
accounting, life sentence as it
elapses—belt loose on a belly

telling everyone what she did
and what will come of it. Two
pink lines, third time around.

WEEK 6 (Landscape with Baby and Dog)

She leaves the door ajar, but the next one opens
onto a barren steppe where the only thing standing
is a shipwrecked marionette, headless and rigged,
that casts no shadow and can't keep its thighs together.

She stands on the rumpled rug, but her feet are already
filthy with the grit that has blown over them and caught
in her cuffs. Stormclouds thicken, and the lone patch
of clear sky is soon overtaken by sulphurous drifts.

She holds the child steady, his rump hanging over
her arm beneath a clutch of capable fingers, but
he scowls, slobbers on her shoulder, his lumpy brow
tensing with grievances about her refusals, her smell.

She wears a tidy cap with blue florets like his. They
are kin. Some angry thing has shredded her smock,
gouged her front and exposed a sagging teat, but the worst
of the pain has passed and she doesn't remember.

You would never put yourself where the sand levels
the landscape, choosing instead to show your face
on the Pekingese about to pounce out of the picture,
whose pert wag boasts of better judgment and bones.

Week 7 (Figure)

A blue line buoys the body up,
wends through breasts, descends
to a shadow that shackles an ankle,

circles a belly big as a hubcap
and overfull of her own blood
plus half-again its volume. She

is bolt upright to balance it,
clutching the caning of a straight-
backed chair, staring into the fear

and a fate still young, ready to jump
if someone lobs her the keys.
Or maybe she's seen it before,

and the mirror in the corner is
a transom to an interior, profile
of an older self, where another

branch of that blue line delivers
oxygen to a nostril. Or maybe
it's not that dire, only a flash

forward to one of the small failures,
when she was sorry she turned
and scolded her for being afraid.

Week 8 (Organogenesis)

On her pedestal outside
the anatomy archives
she is the female form

without skin or fat,
the body as achievement,
indisputable iron,

beauty of the thing.
Body as evidence,
instruction, use,

exposing the means
by which the cords
of the neck engage

as the arm lifts,
the iliac crest
dictates the flank.

The body as idea
without ornament.
Yet even without

a surface—no cheek,
no blush, no smile—
the under-muscle of her

thigh seems to slip
through a parted robe,
the shoulder to shrug,

the heel to dangle
like a sandal. How far
are we from flaying?

Week 9 (Fear)

Two lines lead her astray:
one descends from the neck,

bisects the breast and falls plumb
to the floor, another cuts

an oblique from cheek to sternum,
crossing her body as it blurs

the borders beyond it, marking
her manner: crease, pierce, smudge.

She whites out one lens
of her glasses, steadies the slash

she's drawn across herself,
tacking back with the syntax

of fear—what could these hands
be capable of? She paints

them painting but the fingers
seem to sharpen, fingers made

for darning needles, or a harp,
for the puncture and swivel

of the compass point, the one
swipe it takes to erase a face.

Week 10 (Figure)

She counterbalances her body
weight against the child's
as he tugs toward the low black
tree line beyond her shoulder.
Long fingers, attenuations—
each tendon sustains the hold.
Their skins are chafed
with sunburn and prickly heat.
She paces the length
of the pasture to wear out
another elongated evening.

Week 11 (Trade Routes)

Who gave you the right to click your heels
across museum tile, your notebook balanced
on your forearm like an expert waiter's tray,
while I sleep in my frozen cell, one more
display? Though years of glacial ice expand
and crack the marrow lodes, I'm well preserved,
unearthed fresh as an artichoke. They brought
me back. I felt the slosh of brine inside
the cargo bay, where blood and limbs began
to thaw.

                Like all the rest you jot and list:
turmeric, curry, camphor, nutmeg, myrrh, a dust
of pectin to prevent the rot of snuff or coriander
under glass. I'm yet another name you might
collect, a stenciled placard, *Boy of Teshik Tash,*
the region hatched in red, where minerals and
malachite are mined, the rhomboids fringed
with silver hairs like magnets drawing pins.

Come, caress my acorn skull, my tomb
of stag's horns crossed and tied to weave
a dome, a basket overturned. Reach through
the halo of my shivered sleep and stroke
this fur papoose, this crypt. I am your brother.
Bone spokes fasten a vise around my neck.

Week 12 (Figure)

That breast—worse than an udder,
a gasket, a squeezable tap like a tube
for frosting. On her lap, the children

are dressed in christening gowns
with ribbons to match the veins
in their skulls, alien craniums

that testify she hissed them to sleep.
She croons, disapproves, illum-
inates them in a lead-white halo

that leaves scars on their wrists,
hypoxic faces. She gave, they drank,
she made them pawns, droids, dis-

integrating torsos pasted to wallpaper
or wandering off. She is kinetic,
schizophrenogenic, she is the mama

who makes the mind fray. Her black
shawl drags. Behind them all,
on the wall, a livid red bears down.

Week 13 (Blue Reading)

The logic of a skirt: make solid what is split.

A nail slides under the seal, breaking it. The temptation to scan for an answer without allowing any mitigating greeting

to interfere. Another surface skids over it, crosshatches the hands that hold the letter, drops a scrim over the image, or it's a mesh to stiffen plaster. The temptation to start reading

into it. She's carrying low. A girl, say the market women. Coming to term and the pressure of the skull is between her legs.

Scratch that. At this resolution, the fibers are a graft of dashes, perforated exposures. What sifts through the sienna scrim. A form, a silhouette, that gives no sign other than its solidity, other than the inference of a body within a body, upside down.

What sifts through the scrim

is revision—a smock with loop closures, trimmed at the back to bring in the shape, rid it of flippancy. She steadies the picture like a column, broader at the base. Aligned with orthogonals, a body

absorbed. A cloth to wick away moisture. A woman

in front of a map, opening a letter. She'll take it standing. He or she has responded to her recent letter. Refused to answer the question put to him or her in the earlier letter. Other matters. Instructions, regrets. Several days of uncomfortable travel in her condition. Resist

the temptation to catch her in an expository net. The pixels
suggest a screen full of static, a square of gauze. She is adept at
reading the gaps, whether apertures or silences. A scrim drops,
obscuring the hands that hold the paper,

crosshatching the clarity. A cut at the corner of the mouth that the
tongue keeps touching. When lit from behind. The map comes
down to her shoulders—olive and ochre deltas, an isthmus inferred
from the contours. How eager the mapmaker was to enlarge
the projection to the corners, in spite of inaccuracies, bulbous
distortions. Her hair-band, a tributary. He enlarges

the map by a few centimeters and brings it nearer to the nail-head
chair, which blocks the figure from the viewer, isolates her. Her
stance

implies absorption, repels absorption. This time,

he makes it tone on tone. No depiction, no undertaking. If she is
doing something, the crumpled tablecloth obscures it. Box, book,
pearls, satchel. Speculation

on sequence is hazardous. Any attempt to calculate the cost of
delivery in guilders. The temptation

to scratch the surface. A body beneath the drapes, about to be
split. Scratch that. Annul. A scratched surface, an open weave, a
change of scenery. She is about

to enter her confinement. She scans the page. A map, a scrim
falls, a mesh to stiffen plaster. She is of two minds, reading

into the ostensible welcome, into the aperture, silence.

II.

Week 14 (Suburban Chagall)

She's the figure on the fringe
with her eye on the prophet and loss,

wishing he'd hurry up and finish
his anguished prayer, tourmaline orbits

opening over the heads of the witnesses
as they exit the scene up a circus ladder,

the doves huddling beneath a mule
beneath a backlit citron crucifixion,

everybody in town hoping he'll come-to
coherent enough to proffer some word

on what happened and whether or not
it's still safe to take the train.

She's watching, intent on a shoulder
that might be a mountain, ferned and sheer,

that might be heaving over her,
her fear fading into a faint stipple

in the grisaille, an ochre overlay—
a forehead rubbed with a thumb

before the dust gets in. She holds
her baby facing front, the way you do

when they start to get heavy.
If he hears her or wavers, he gives

no sign, thrusts his star-singed hand
into another godforsaken flame.

Week 15 (Quickening)

Scraps of story cycle over an olive grid—
above it a face turns up to sing skyward,
to stitch the images in sequence without cause,

fantail, fish lure, finger puppet fantasies
of holster and rocket, wild oats and tricky
whiskers, a landscape broken down into boxes

—moss green, slate, mulch—to offset
the mauve doughiness of a human shape.
A caller, neither marionette nor caricature,

announcer of the pathos of *Fruchtbarkeit*,
of fruit and small fry, arms upraised, praising
the patchwork, navel flattened to a smudge.

First flutter of movement (a bubble erupts
under a gloved hand). I lean in, listen
for signs of life—yes, listen—quiet all else

to hear that inner touch, that thump.
Blind crier, the belly is a book in a book,
the spine cracked so you can see clear through.

I live as much with the dead as with the unborn,
somewhat closer to the heart of creation
than usual, but not nearly close enough.

Does warmth emanate from me? Coolness?
Beyond all ardor there is nothing to discuss.
Face down on the belly, the book jumps.

Somewhat closer to the belly of utterance
than usual, but just out of earshot. *Beyond*
all ardor there is nothing to discuss.

Week 16 (Highchair)

A child of wax, nylon, and twine in a highchair,
his charred head tossed back in tantrum,

limbs stumped and sticky with cobweb.
No doubt someone tried to spoon offending mashes

into those decay-pocked cheeks.
You've done it yourself. Just one more bite.

Just sit there until you stop screaming.
He was having one of his rages,

the woman told 20/20, so she put him in a highchair
in an unfinished part of the basement,

but the chair, top-heavy, flipped from his
thrashing. The investigation later found

she had fixed him there with duct tape,
that he died from suffocation, not the blow

to the head. She sits, touching fingertips,
and the kitchen wallpaper behind her head repeats:

checks and roosters, alternating squares
of blue and gold that frame each bird, reverse.

Week 17 (Three Girls)

You linger at the rail, all ringlets and scratches,
sending up shrieks while the boys hurtle themselves
headlong off the slides, glancing over your shoulders

to watch us watching because you know already
how the onlookers take stock, size up, surmise.
He has seen you too: three girls along a road

that intersects a whitewashed seawall. The first,
bareheaded with a black sash, is the one
with vision. The girl in the red kerchief, repentant.

The third, aloof. Your bodies form a trapezoid
that leans against the grain of plank and pile.
In a few years the three of you will cut class

and stand if not along the Aasgaardstrand
then someplace else where you can turn your backs
on a picturesque little harbor, peering down

at the shadow of three linden trees that share
a common crown, thinking about the old choices—
the rocks in the pocket, the road back to town.

Week 18 (Word of Mouth)

Not traffic but the pace of traffic, marking time

while the women circle the block, feeling in their purses for change, counting the minutes they intend to spend. She sets it down

block by block, cell by cell. Shale. Vinegar. Canola. Moleskin. Not an axis, not an intersection. She smudges the corners, shades the periphery with a gray wash. The women

make sentences all morning long. Without a doubt. When it comes down to it. She's the one whose son. From one mouth

to the next. Gossip as inoculation: not us, not us. Not cobblestone, gingko leaf, gutter. Not darkened windows. From one block

to the next, searching for metered spots. Dixon. Neperan. Main. Depeyster. No single droplet makes it all the way down the windshield before it intersects, accumulates, splits. She sets them down

one after another. Creases that cut into the array from the top, tilting the planes. Not misaligned zipper teeth. Not a harbor. Not getting anywhere in this traffic today. Not the patches where the defroster is not working. Not the vantage of an unseen height. Not a word but word

of mouth. The women deduce. A gasp does not count as a breath. Would never leave the cap. Would never assume. Word spreads,

a pinprick, a momentary twinge. The sweet aftertaste of voyeurism. Not corrugations exposed at the rip in the carton. Not rivulets, not haze. Not a filament, not a fuse. The women count them on their fingers,

the other women's sons. Age two, choking. Age six, drowning. Age thirty-one, suicide. In each case the mouth is full.

The women look up at the clock, about to run, about to expire, counting them as they pass

Ray's Optic. Maurice Lacroix. Mi Bohio. Joy Deluxe. Silver Tips. Coffee Labs. Hope Hose. Elysian Fields. Bellas. Caravela. Hank's Alley. Good Karma. Cherry Door. Mint. Black. Blue. White.

Black. White. Aqua. Yellow. Magenta. Black. White. Black. Olive. Black. Copper. Black. White. Black. White. White. Black. White. Maroon. Aqua. Yellow. Black. White. Black. Olive. Black. Copper. Black. White. Black. White. Gray.

Week 19 (White Vertical Water)

Maybe her grief ascends like this,
a breath indrawn and then released

so the bubbles rise to the top, break
and curlicue under, scrolling back down

the airless columns where they coil
and settle among the sirens,

early March, a Monday night.
She thought he'd walk to the corner,

no farther. Circumstance dissolves
like this, like colorless powder,

or flattens, white on white, into shapes
instead of stories. Scissors would do it—

drops and diamonds cut from strips
of white paper, patterns traced

from the bottoms of containers,
scallops and waves, bright rows

of peaks from pinking shears.
The dog shook on the bank,

drenched, dragging the leash.
White, vertical, the story lifts

the way a drinking straw,
after the bubbles surround it,

lifts out of the glass.
The box divides in thirds,

then ninths, channels of white
under the ice, too thin to hold

the weight of ovals, thumbnails,
imprints of palms, rolling

down cold white columns.
The divers from Dobbs Ferry

put on their headlamps and found him,
thirty feet out, thirty feet down.

Week 20 (Middle Distance)

Call it cure or call it quack
operation to excise stones

from the head, it's supervised
by a sheep-faced nun who's also
the scrub nurse ready with razor,
retractor, screw. It takes place
oddly out of doors, overcast.

She props her elbow on a café table
with a fig for a base, the book
on her head, sending up science
and sanctity with a tattered scroll:

Lubbert das Gelded Badger
slung in a chair, drunk and bloated
while they bore inches into him.

The moral's in the middle distance—
pigeons, litter, a cathedral spire
you might call Mylar, mutter
about meaning (futility of worldly

healing). She smirks—pity
about all that. As for the afterlife,
there's still nowhere to sit.

WEEK 2

Just as the e

merely a biological fact one percent of

was in me when I w

if one were inscribed determined by on

half a sign, all the eg

working accept that each girl is transito

now, weighting down t

refuse by all means have a child but st

or the six ripening avo

deny don't have children clarified eth

shape the same as t

ruin your art abandon has manifest on

their sheen t

should get to work peers critics begs t

spa

till Life)

.t made her
thers who leave their side impact
n, half a daughter,
ther an obstacle to the work not
'll ever have are in her
wning achievement is constructed
ter, solid as river stones
one interruption more significant
es in this still life, their
n't live the suburban life emergence
ket that frames them,
nmetry reluctant chose not to have
ne as the empty
estion of who merely a biological fact
ween.

Week 22 (Anacoluthon)

a stray minute to look again

> at Dubuffet's picture of childbirth, where a woman

interrupted by whimpers, then wails

> lies naked on a bed, flanked with institutional blue

across my lap, attempting to write with one

> chafed flesh, pink as an eraser, the chalky outline of her body sets off

an index of disturbed coherence, detours

> through a thick layer of green that

wrings his mottled hands as if casting a spell

> just as Dubuffet said—there's no great difference between the paste he spread and a cat or trout

screaming in spite of his recent feed

> the woman clings to the canvas, the hole that has just become the birth canal

makes it impossible to finish this

> baby between her legs, his penis pointing toward

dream in which a breast sloughs off

        while the husband stands by looking distressed

by the milk that must be

        getting hot in there, in his tweed, wishing he

moment of quiet, a moment

        drawn in crayon with crude symmetry

the dryer clicks as the snaps of his small garments toss in the cylinder

        suggesting a calm the scarred surface belies

WEEK 23 (Exposure)

Not a baby but a block of wood.

Cradle it. Press your hand to your breast as if angling a nipple into its mouth.

A whitewashed stable in a resort town, off season. She sets up a long exposure, arranges the froth of cheap tulle. Hands stained not with dye but with odor—garlic, or fish. A picture

of contentment. *Hold the pose,*

gaze through the gauze. Reasonable fee for the afternoon. A piece of hair loosens,

then itches. *Hold the pose.* She clears her throat, softens the focus on the hollow of an ear, rearranges

the drapes, swaths of white cut from a tablecloth. *Tuck your feet under. Turn your cheek toward the light. Steady,*

tip your cheek toward me. Think

of something else: a fallen star your milk sustains. A whole soured gallon poured down the sink. A bit of machinery,

a mishap. She rigs it so the blaze of sun comes from the right, stipples the surface of pillar and trough. Beam, sash, cistern. A cache of wrappers in the chimney corner, swept of ash.

Cradle it. Gaze through the veil. A swaddled block. Stiff baby. Skid baby. Jostle baby.

Tightens a wing-nut. That errant tendril. *Grit your teeth, bid your hair stand up,*

think of other things. A man on a mechanic's roof, a unisex salon, saplings wrapped in burlap.

A flashbulb, a fallen flare. Floaters in the visual field, bits of burnt retina.

Breath beneath the netting. Stifle the urge to. Bridal bridle. Heat on the neck, under the arms. Plank baby. Balsa-wood baby. Rolled-up-towel baby. Bale-of-hay baby. Scarecrow baby. Pipe baby. Suppress

a gesture. Wood baby.

Would you. Wooden leg. Would have seen it coming. Wooed. Sold. Shouldered. Soldier. Soldered. Shudder. Shutter. Shudder in the loins,

sheet of aluminum, flammable blue, a flare. Satisfied

the taste of wealthy clients. Reproduced. A few cents an hour for a few hour's work. *Your milk,*

milk white. Milk teeth. Milk duds. Milky way. No use crying over. Crybaby. Cry, baby. Flinch, flinch at the flash,

this fallen star your milk sustains. Milk. Milk it

for all it's worth.

Week 24 (Viability)

about to squirm out of her grasp

    fidget with the coverlet climb
    over the loge

        she may not have intended

a fine fringe

    about to unravel about to squeeze
    the sponge over his pudgy back

        she may not have intended to return

bracing her knee to restrain his
                      arch away

about to skid off the porch

    soil the gabardine

she may not have intended to return
to the theme but did so under

                pull him away from the edge

the dual pressure of critical praise
and a favorable market

            sling him back

    about to wail gag grab

restrain the impulse

                             to hold him

               after its success established the motif
               so firmly as her hallmark

clasp his wrist

                     about to swat the hand

     hold his face in the water
     glass as he bites the rim

under the dual pressure

                     cupping his chin so it won't quaver

so he won't move

Week 25 (Biopsy)

Vigilance and irritation that don't let up
for an instant—even when we invent
a spiral staircase for suburbanites rising
from brick and timber houses, sailing over
the hydrangeas like fireflies released
from a dairy case—even when we improvise
an air of celestial silhouettes, because face it

we're just shifting our weight curbside
with our eyes on the toddlers, ready
to grip a wrist when a car comes by,
ready to stencil ivy on the electric box
out of sheer boredom, hanging on
to their wrists while they yank and whine
then letting go until the next car comes—

even when we pause our ceaseless talk
about why this or that has caused this or that
tantrum, nightmare, hangnail, rash,
to squint at the streetlights until a halo forms,
to trace a helix heavenward for Jessica
who chose to have both breasts removed.

Week 26 (St. Rage's Vault)

Here are your instructions: go down to a strip mall
in Odenton, Maryland, and find a sparrow nesting
in the G of the ST RAGE VAULT. Don't bother
looking for the O. By touch, locate the pressure valve

and release the lock. You'll know me at once—
I am the bone-white drum, the tauter-than-taut
membrane of the throat. I'm the cigar, the celebrity,
the troll beneath the bridge and tollbooth collector,
the rabid paw and the hundred needles sunk in your gut.

You will lie awake nights and remember we're not
talking about safety deposit boxes sacheted and lined
with blue velvet, we're talking about burial alive.
Repeat after me: two spaces after a period, one

after a comma. Lose a tooth, put it in milk. If
stabbed, don't pull out the knife. No bronze booties,
prom corsages, only casks and torchlight. I am
mitered and vinegared. Here is the church, lay
your damp cheek against the pew—acres of black

you rehearsed every young rage. Given the choices,
take shelter here—where brains marinate in broth,
where you can nibble on dubious mushrooms,
jackhammer your teeth to bits. A bit is an eighth

of a dollar. In New Orleans the dead rot fast
in tombs hot as bread ovens. Handkerchiefs
come in handy. The phrenic nerve refers pain
to the shoulder, white fiber inside an orange rind.
I'm the one who sounds the alarm, snatches away

packages you never meant to steal, shakes you
by the wrist until you hold yourself accountable.
Persist. Open another. I can only lick the stamp.
Coyote anagrams to oocyte. Pull the thread until

the vault unravels, detonates the eye of the needle
so that somewhere the lily horizes. Make up
any verbs you'd like. Look around for a button
that will launch the ejection seat. Close cover
before striking. This is not an ode, Dr. Manly.

The eggshell grit between your teeth sets you
transmitting like a crystal radio, frequencies so high
you hear yourself talking about millennial poetry,
blackjack odds, and almanacs. Prepare, cover

your head. The rage will overtake you in a wave,
pesticide fog from the mosquito truck, a routine
you've practiced since you were fetal. I'd shrug,
if I could. In the end it's a matter of detritus—
caught in the gravel, the orange bits of fish shit

are the mad erasures of a paragraph. Be sure you've
proofed and capitalized the names of the dead,
mastered the rules of grammar, the finer points
of meter. Put another coin in the meter, I'll tell you

why I was canonized: a girl with a sandy scalp
goes down a waterslide, catches her straddle on a seam
in the fiberglass and splits herself apart. Speed,
the nylon rip, menarche and libation, aqua blue.
Sketch the vectors, it happened. Or there's the boy:

a hammock peg snaps off, he cracks his skull, and
while his face begins to warp and swell, I summon
my networks Georgia to Maine. Before he dies,
he sees their prayers alight in arcs of dashes, cities

bursting into daisies of intercontinental missiles.
Ah yes, the freak tanning-booth accident. Teen feels
dizzy, walks home. Her mother comments on her
rancid sweat. She lies down, dead in an hour, cooked.
I am her patron saint. Forget the Dewey Decimal.

Grope as they did in Waco for the buried school bus
with a week's worth of air. Offer suet to the sparrow.
But cut the whimpers. For the love of God, Fortunato,
bellow with rage, become aware of the smell of your
own breath. Go ahead, try, rub me back into the lamp.

III.

III

Week 27 (Figure)

No globe, no fruit—only
the redundancy of her desire.

Reclining nude in the corner
of the couch, one fist loose

at her chin, the other a pivot
on her hip, she levels her gaze

with half-smirk and smolder
the way she does every morning

on the train when strangers
lay their hands on her body.

Week 28 (Stone Child)

Two souls in one body, one body
    within another, the fecund body
and its fact: a seven-month fetus.

The woman is ninety-two, the fetus
    a freak of nature, a rare finding
reported in the literature by Drs. Speiser

and Brezina of Vienna—a child
    of stone, a *lithopaedion*, carried for
sixty years, its tissues infiltrated

with salts, its membranes spared.
    She must have known it stilled,
settled into a space and heft, something

to carry across a field of fear, another
    of loss, until her late admission
for pneumonia when the mass was

discovered, measured, entered into
    the archive. She must have known
it was alive, and then not, and then,

crudely, a story someone would write up
    for the county, murmuring
about the latest laughter, slaughter.

She crossed a century, and at the end
    were means to peer into a body,
no longer opaque but still encrypted,

a half-tone image of storms across a stone
    skull. She must have sensed its odd
propulsion, irregular time, an urgency

she could not countermand. She must have
    faced the fall with dread, unable to
imagine reprisal or compromise because

there was none, only the inexorable
    onset of what would begin
with a twinge. So it began. An episode

of acute pain, after which an expanse
    of years unmarked by serious illness
until the present, final case. A slur

in the quick rhythm of valve and pulse,
    a dream of clotted colors pulled from
its mouth—kite tail of improbable scarves.

Week 29 (Goodnight Nobody)

She's not whispering, she's muttering
shut up. Don't be fooled by geometry,

linear perspective from corner to corner,
foreground broadening into a stage apron

where lamplight, compass-drawn, cuts
a transverse swath of green. She left

her knitting needles on the seat, put
prongs on the swags that flank the fire,

and teeth are missing from that comb—
she went after your scalp, and she's likely

to do so again. Don't let yourself slide
into the casual *mise en abîme*, the picture

in the picture in the picture of the same
superlunary bovine, the road that goes off

the edge of the woodcut into an unknown
town and you bet it's not Bethlehem, mush

curdling in the bowl, the black phone
ringing with a wrong number at four.

Shut your eyes. Dream. Your mama
wears fisherman's waders and tonight,

my sweet, one of those swampish trees,
brittle and diseased, is coming down.

WEEK 30 (Maternity Bathing Suit)

Forget those gilded mamas,
she's a magic marker Venus de Milo

at the open swim, a cellulite bird
of blub and doodles full of words,

A-E-I-O-U and growing
a varicose cosmos

of pantihoseless possibility,
up to her anatomy in irregular stars,

her daisy-decal polka-dot
pliant bingo bottom buoyant enough

to balance an elephantine arabesque
off the ladder, smile

at mister-smug-one shrunk
in his trunks in front of

her flagrant magenta bellyful
of flutter kicks—O shaky bravura—

and drop, splashless,
into water over her head.

WEEK 31 (Chaos Blame Trust)

Words he wanted to know, yesterday, while I double-knotted his shoes.

A line of rising water, a rotted couch, a coastline with infinite inlets, the arms of the storm as they lash the map, tracks turning back for some path but finding none, a globe spun, a finger put down to stop it: that's Sumatra, that's the Fertile Crescent.

Generators brought in to backlight the podium, to ensure, promote, mortar recruit checkpoint counsel curfew fallout roadside scatter fired into a mosque. Shrapnel delta fray. Fallujah. Samarra. A woman in her twenties slumped in a cowering position shot in the back of the neck.

Home: saturated, blackened. Evacuations along the overpass, a matter of days before. Hunched under rafters, he waited for a helicopter with only a quart of. A police launch, circling back to mark. Caught in the outboard. Cots on the sidewalk, radicals in the outer atmosphere, errant cells and cuts, counterterror, outcasts, ire, flood, fire, debris of leaflets, feces, oil, curves that stir the surface of the river after rain.

Home: dishes, spit-up dreadlocks in the baby's hair, rusted rack and pinion.

Home: on whose shoulders, on whose knees, under what circumstances, under what conditions, understanding, upstanding, upending, ending, render, reprimand, rent, remind.

Home: your great-grandfather, age sixteen, was playing hockey with six other boys when the ice cracked and the whole group fell through. Nearest to the bank, he pulled five boys to safety, one after another with a branch, but he could not reach the last, who was his brother, could not, then or ever, go home.

Outcasts, ire, flood, fire, debris of leaflets, feces, oil.

Week 32 (Willow Grove, Pennsylvania, 1931)

At some point he must have turned and left
his brother under the ice, entered a warm room
and taken off his wet things. He would assume
the papers got the story right, the lake under drifts
of late snow, the number of boys playing hockey
(seven), the number he pulled to safety (five),
hand over hand with a branch, the one survived
by parents, sisters, a brother who had been lucky

enough to be near the muddy bank, who later left
the seminary before he took his vows, left
his wife when their sons were small, tried to atone
for it after a decade, to pick up where they left
off—left the door ajar, left the light on, left
the reception for a smoke, left well enough alone.

Week 33 (Weaning the Christ)

The cherub shoulders a gun
while the Virgin works out the kinks
in the plan, weighs the meanings

of redeemable objects—
spigot, spindle, rug over a barrel.

She shifts him to the other side
but he squirms, starts kicking
the folds of her skirt.
He wants to walk. Soon,

to make him a god-made-man,
she'll have to get him off the sauce.
Meanwhile she waits for

letdown, long seconds
when he sucks but nothing comes,
his mouth strong with purpose
on the brink of a wail, one fist

whirling, punching
a jammed candy machine,

until the tension gathers like a drawstring—
fullness shot through with sting.

Week 34 (Wired)

Stare before it shorts out, trips and fizzes
dim, before the clattery glass can cross

the room and cool—a belle, a bride in bulbs

with a linguini train, an incandescent teapot
rat-trap clown-coat grapevine ghost.

Make it up to me! Filaments, a fitting

end, a fragile frock of udders, Christmas-
colored bodies of balloon dachshunds,

bound to pop, but no—they're brittle,

not one would bounce. For the face,
a wire cage, for the wrists, two clamps,

an O-ring to rope it up.

Turn it on, take it off, take it over,
turn it up—let me help you

with that switch.

Surely you are not surprised
such brightness would be so heavy?

Surely you are not too hot

and shy to smile? Careful now.
Let me help you with that switch.

Week 35 (Mothership)

It's there as soon as I close my eyes, masts tilting in the haze. On the edges of vision the transformer towers for the railroad are a lattice against the sky—fretwork, filaments. The light flattens and folds itself like an origami bird.

A peacock, flexing the oily rainbow of its neck.

Max was three and afraid of it. All birds scared him—pigeons on the sidewalk, brown sparrows beneath a picnic table. Once a rooster at a petting zoo had pecked his hand, its cockscomb swinging beneath its chin like a scrotum. That day by the river, Max saw the peacock crossing the lawn and let out a cry of rage.

I picked him up and pointed toward the water. Look, boat. A clipper ship was coming around the bend, tacking back and forth across the wide part of the Hudson north of the Tappan Zee. A ship for the tourist season, a four-hour cruise. Or for pirates, or for purgatory, or for a black prince.

It was a hot day but Max refused to get in the water. It was too furry, he said. It had onions in it. So we dug a trench on the little beach, a crescent of pebbly sand in the cove near the marina.

After a while a boy about his age arrived with his nanny, who emptied a large bag of buckets and hoes and sifters onto the sand between them. Max set his jaw and straightened his legs in front of him, trying to block the other child from his ditch, which the boy began kicking. The nanny guided her charge aside and in the same deft gesture pulled a toddler to her hip. She had her own daughter with her that day, she explained, who was almost two.

The three children played and fought. There was only one green shovel. Throwing rocks was not allowed. The peacock is more afraid of you. The nanny picked small pieces of glass out of the sand and deposited them in a pile on top of the retaining wall. She chatted. Her name was Lucimer. She had been watching the boy since he was a baby. She was obliged to bring her own daughter with her to work that day because she couldn't—the boys began to throw sand and she interfered—she had been obliged to bring her own daughter to work with her that day because her sister-in-law, who usually watched her, had to take her son to Emergency with a ruptured eardrum. She looked at her watch. Her boss usually took an early train home on Fridays and didn't like the daughter to be there—conflict of interest. She sat the little girl down and handed her a cup.

It was overcast, but there was a glare off the river. When I squinted into it, the light tilted into planes—glass tiles scored with a blade and cracked clean along a line.

The nanny turned to me. She needed to call her sister-in-law to see if she was back, could I watch the kids for a minute while she went to the payphone on the train platform?

The clipper ship was closer now, flying a flag from the crow's nest.

The other boy got hot and began to splash at the edge. Max hesitated, then followed. The little girl toddled over and picked up the shovel. Then they were up to their chests. They wobbled, shrieked. The ship passed and the wake sent small waves flapping into them. Max lunged and I grabbed him by the elbow, pulled him up as his chin slipped in. A swim-ring floated by, the inflatable kind with the head of a seahorse or chicken. Both boys reached for it, tugging it between them. I held the slippery ring as best I could with one hand while each of them took a turn, keeping the other child within an arm's reach. Their bodies slick and turning, spinning in the ring, all elbows and bellies, reddening shoulder blades. Turning and plunging, within an arm's reach.

I looked up and scanned the beach for the little girl.

Signal wires on the horizon, strung on the X-girders of the radio towers. Parallels that skew and split into fowl and fern, into the calico triangles of an unassembled quilt. The geometries shifted, checkered perspective upriver while the light slid down.

The gate to the dock had been left open.

Light skid off the surfaces—tangled skeins of sun and shade. Ferns in a chain-link fence. A bird.

When her body was found, the back of her pink bathing suit was puffed with a pocket of air.

Lucimer, light of the sea. Calling. Checking the port-a-potties and the parking lot. The jetty, under the picnic tables. There was a Gatorade bottle filled with sand, holding down a checked tablecloth. A clipper ship headed downstream, toward the city. Lucimer, her forehead fighting terror. Lucimer stooping to pick up the boy's sandals, hooking each over a finger. Lucimer, her mouth still forming thanks.

The Yankee clipper, its masts disappearing downriver toward the dock it shared with Circle Line. The peacock, strutting over the pedestrian bridge. Light that tessellates, tilts, folding itself along the lines of time.

Lucimer, light of the sea. A few days after it happened I slipped into the back of St. Teresa's right before the service started. I don't think she saw me when she passed the pew and I don't know what I would have said to her if she had, or even if I had thought about the possibility, or if I could think at all. She was clutching a piece of loose-leaf paper with some ballpoint writing on it. I fled.

Week 36 (Figure)

Dislocations and recovery, aftershocks—
you are not aware of your shoulders when you are in labor,
so I left the shoulders out.

The face tries to float free, but the arms
sling the chin to catch it. She is red-handed.
There are pansies, staunching bandages,

sheets that crumple into a relief map.
Most of the light seems to leak out
as the breasts become engorged,

areolas like blackened pancakes.
No bellwether of metamorphosis, only slack surprise
that the eyes reveal the effort while the mouth

smears featureless, that the womb
could go from globe to grapefruit in a matter of hours,
that the baby would be gone so long.

Week 37 (Tachycardia)

The night the staccato started in my chest
      we rode the plains of plasticine Nebraska.
We were cycloptic, fiber-optic—fifty-percent-off
      and Dentyne clean, riding a wild steed
that bares its teeth, your arm yanked out
      like a shank steak. You said, Bev,
it's Splenda, it's Allegra, it's Extra Virgin,
      the last ride of the suburban sublime,
a race from disgrace trailing juices and glue,
      gristle and tentacle, putty and pox,
the beast's flank shimmering like the quilted silver
      of the chuckwagon. You said, it's All
Free and Clear—a money-back one-track satisfaction
      guarantee. You in your jodhpurs and spurs, me
in my giddy-pink housedress with poky nipples.
      You said, buy now, Bev, for limited time,
and I rubbed the grit from your eyes. We
      quaked and bellyached, flashing past
this taxi-cab-maxi-pad-not-so-bad latest fad,
      a fly-off-the-handle fight or flight for LOVE.
Bev and Bernie, lucky and lemon-lime, ready
      to short-circuit and fray, getting it going on
on a gelding, fast as toast. We were wrung out
      and strung out, stung with rug-burn, burning
both ends. You said, you are my Sunday raisin,
      my Tuesday tonsil, my bronco, my best
Dakota sweet-tooth, duchess, don't you go.
      When it was dawn we hadn't slept at all.

The next night the staccato kept at it.
      You tracked mud on the linoleum, tracked in
the thoughts my thoughts left behind—
      motion, marrow, roe. You lolled
around with your lasso and saffron sideburns,

    torpid and corpulent, busting your chops.
You said, don't get so lonesome, Lindsey Lohan,
    have a gum jump rope and a blue-
raspberry slush. Try Pledge, try Soft Scrub,
    and if that won't take it out, try Tide.
I said, Bernie, you see the world through the rose-
    colored Plexiglas of the conversion van,
and all you want is flat on my back with my feet
    on the carpeted ceiling. I almost slid under,
a high five of saliva across the sky. Songs
    started up in the spaces the thoughts
left behind, jingles and jukebox tunes, the deputy
    and the liar, crackling with static. I said,
only a sublime of self-disgust can save art
    from narcissism. I said, I don't
suppose I'll be able to fill this hole in my soul
    with cornflakes. You said, Choke back
the cherry expectorant—mercy!—expect to die.

When it was dawn I hadn't slept at all. The next
    night neither. The fourth night I slipped
inside my body and saw it from the inside out,
    incisor roots writhing out of the gums,
slug tongues, nematodes and notochords, nerves
    that lead back from the retina, singed with
sunspots, lipids lunging through the livewires
    of my limbs. That rapping—that's my heart,
that hyperfast rasp. You said, gimme a sign, a guide
    to this guacamole grotesque, before I say
uncle umbilical and split, right down the middle.
    I said, a diet of awe will not nourish long.
You put your finger on it, a pound of raw chuck
    with a pulse, a piston, this piston-driven
heart. This tacky, tacky heart. I felt my tastebuds
    rising up to meet my mouth. Wake up,
Bernie, shake awake and stand up. Don't sleep,
    Bernie, don't leave me alone with this
ratta-tatta rickshaw lockjaw rat-trap of a mind.

Week 38 (Figure)

She lets the afternoon lapse.
A gate blocks the way out
of the kitchen. Together,
they are shapes among
the shapes through which
the window cuts the sun.
She is partially effaced.
The child is fixated with
frantic passion on a bobby
sock that won't stay on.
She stares at something
several stories down.

Week 39 (Blue Nudes)

As if she were a rind pulled back

from a dried-out fruit, crouching with her face on her knees, her flesh etched and streaked, as if she were disconsolate or

drowned, bobbing by the moorings in a yolky light, her head dropping below her shoulders

as if bending to wash, a breast hanging beneath her like a bag of coins, one day shy

of a year since she saw him last, naked on the settee, ready to yield to the shadows, the leaf and shag, as if she were

found dead, fifty feet from the berm between the quarry and the neighborhood, her skin mottled and bruised

as if he gripped her so the flesh blanched, then suffused again with deeper pink, as if

she heard someone come in downstairs and set her book down on the bed,

cornered, her body a curve to contrast the entablature, as if she were

woken in the blue hour, sweating cold, rising again to attend to a cry,

exposed, only an arm to shield herself, or

cut, torso from limbs, then scissored into shapes—megaphone, hambone, fortune cookie, tadpole, melon, drumstick, udder, fin— her body printed in error, pressed with punctuation, a nipple and a navel, as if she were

turning an ear toward the door, letting her mind stray

into the afternoon, into an old argument, as if she were

opening her mouth to speak, starting to form

an answer to an unasked question, as if she were

ready to get out and towel off, reconsider, reach over

to straighten the lamp, catch a glimpse of herself in the globe, as if she were

about to sit up, remember the time, refuse, seize

the pieces scattered on the sideboard, gather her hair again in a quick twist, as if she were

opening her mouth to absorb the shadow and press it into syllables, ready

to get off her knees, rub out the stiffness and steady herself,

stash a few things in a satchel,

shake off the chill, as if

her body were tensing to rise, as if

she set down her book and turned to hear who was coming.

Week 40 (Nocturne)

Newborn, you open these hours
in zigzag chiaroscuro, divide

the night until it's a drawer
of glossy wood, a printer's drawer

with its slots and boxes
half carved out, each square

almost a sound—a partial T,
beveled Ns and Zs,

hooks and knobs, finials,
fluted columns, corners

joined with mortise and tenon,
measures of the darkness,

fugue of nightwork rising
to a cry, rising to run a thumb

over grooves and spindles,
minutes turning the stiles

and synapses, cogs that interlock
to turn the matter, mind.

Your polished eyes
are the only light in this room.

Hewn from darkness,
the minutes rise as you open

your hand to touch the ladder H
and spin it sideways into I.

NOTES

I.

WEEK 1 (Interruption)
Simone Martini, *Annunciation*, 1333, tempera on wood

WEEK 2 (Thought)
Auguste Rodin, *La Pensée*, 1886, marble

WEEK 3 (Arachne: Recent Memory)
Battista Rossi, workshop of Hans Karcher, *Tapestry Depicting Scenes from Ovid's Metamorphoses*, 1545, detail

WEEK 4 (Fabrication)
Louise Bourgeois, *Untitled*, 1996, lithograph, woodcut on paper, with hand coloring

WEEK 5 (Figure)
Alice Neel, *Blanche Angel, Pregnant*, 1937, pastel on paper

WEEK 6 (Landscape with Baby and Dog)
Dorothea Tanning, *Maternity*, 1946, oil on canvas

WEEK 7 (Figure)
Alice Neel, *Margaret Evans Pregnant*, 1978, oil on canvas

WEEK 8 (Organogenesis)
Marion Young, *Essentia*, 1979, bronze

WEEK 9 (Fear)
Alice Bailly, *Self-Portrait*, 1917, oil on canvas

WEEK 10 (Figure)
Alice Neel, *Ginny and Andrew*, 1978, oil on canvas

WEEK 11 (Trade Routes)
Diorama, Gardner D. Stout Hall of Asian Peoples, American Museum of Natural History, New York

WEEK 12 (Figure)
: Alice Neel, *Degenerate Madonna*, 1930, oil on canvas

WEEK 13 (Blue Reading)
: X-ray photograph of Vermeer's *Woman in Blue Reading a Letter*, c. 1662-64

II.

WEEK 14 (Suburban Chagall)
: Marc Chagall, *The Prophet Joel*, c. 1963, stained glass, The Union Church of Pocantico Hills, New York

WEEK 15 (Quickening)
: Paul Klee, *Ventriloquist and Crier in the Moor*, 1923, watercolor and ink on paper. Italicized lines are from Klee's notebooks.

WEEK 16 (Highchair)
: Bruce Conner, *THE CHILD*, 1959-60, wax figure with nylon, cloth, metal, and twine in a highchair

WEEK 17 (Three Girls)
: Edvard Munch, *Girls on a Jetty*, 1918-20, color woodcut and lithograph. This poem is for Josephine Stratman.

WEEK 18 (Word of Mouth)
: Maria Elena Vieira Da Silva, *The Town*, 1955, oil on canvas

WEEK 19 (White Vertical Water)
: Louise Nevelson, *White Vertical Water*, 1972, painted wood, 26 sections. This poem remembers Julian Geach, who drowned in Fremont Pond in Sleepy Hollow, New York, on March 6, 2006. The poem is for Robyn Holden Geach.

WEEK 20 (Middle Distance)
: Hieronymus Bosch, *The Extraction of the Stone of Madness (The Cure of Folly)*, 1475-1480, oil on board

WEEK 21 (Still Life)
: Georgia O'Keefe, *Alligator Pears in a Basket*, 1921, charcoal on paper

WEEK 22 (Anacoluthon)
Jean Dubuffet, *L'Accouchement*, 1944, oil on canvas

WEEK 23 (Exposure)
Gertrude Käsebier, *The Manger*, c. 1899, platinum print. A few lines incorporate phrases from W. B. Yeats's "Mother of God."

WEEK 24 (Viability)
Mary Cassatt, *Mother About To Wash Her Sleepy Child*, 1880, oil on canvas; *Jules Being Dried By His Mother*, 1900, oil on canvas; *Mother and Child (Baby's Back)*, 1889-90, drypoint; *Mother Combing Her Child's Hair*, 1898, pastel and gouache on paper; *Baby with Left Hand Touching a Tub*, 1890-91, pencil and charcoal on paper; *Mother Feeding Her Child*, 1896, pastel. Italicized lines quote the art historian Nancy Mowll Mathews.

WEEK 25 (Biopsy)
Hollis Sigler, *To Kiss the Spirits: Now, This Is What It Is Really Like,* 1993, oil on canvas

WEEK 26 (St. Rage's Vault)
White plastic lettering on one-story brick wall. A few lines echo Richard Hugo's "Flying, Reflying, Farming" and Edgar Allan Poe's "The Cask of Amontillado."

III.

WEEK 27 (Figure)
Alice Neel, *Claudia Bach, Pregnant*, 1975, oil on canvas

WEEK 28 (Stone Child)
Ultrasound image in *The Lancet,* March 1995

WEEK 29 (Goodnight Nobody)
Clement Hurd, illustrations for *Goodnight Moon*, 1947

WEEK 30 (Maternity Bathing Suit)
Niki de Saint-Phalle, *Yellow Nana*, 1993, painted polyester on steel base

WEEK 31 (Chaos Blame Trust)
Video news coverage and video stills, September 2005

WEEK 32 (Willow Grove, Pennsylvania, 1931)
Newspaper photograph of F. Stanley M. Allendorf, drowned February 15, 1931

WEEK 33 (Weaning the Christ)
Albrecht Dürer, *The Sojourn of the Holy Family in Egypt*, 1501-02, woodcut

WEEK 34 (Wired)
Atsuko Tanaka, *Electrical Dress*, 1956, lamps, neon tubes

WEEK 35 (Mothership)
Francesca DiMattio, *Black Ship*, 2006, oil on canvas

WEEK 36 (Figure)
Alice Neel, *Childbirth*, 1939, oil on canvas. Italicized lines are Neel's words.

WEEK 37 (Tachycardia)
Aaron Jackson, *Giddy Up*, 2006, acrylic collage on canvas

WEEK 38 (Figure)
Alice Neel, *Ginny and Elizabeth*, 1976, oil on canvas

WEEK 39 (Blue Nudes)
Pablo Picasso, *The Blue Nude (Seated Female Nude from Behind)*, 1902, oil on canvas; *The Blue Room*, 1901, oil on canvas. Pierre Bonnard, *Blue Nude*, 1899, oil on canvas; *Nude Crouching in the Bath*, 1940, oil on canvas; *Nude in the Bathtub with Small Dog*, 1941-46, oil on canvas. Henri Matisse, *Blue Nude I, II, III*, 1952, gouache-painted paper cut-outs on canvas. Roy Lichtenstein, *Blue Nude*, 1995, oil and magna on canvas.

WEEK 40 (Nocturne)
Louise Nevelson, *Luminous Zag: Night*, 1971, painted wood, 105 boxes

ABOUT THE AUTHOR

B. K. FISCHER'S first book of poems, the novel-in-verse *Mutiny Gallery,* won the 2011 T. S. Eliot Prize. Educated at Johns Hopkins, Columbia, and New York University, she is the author of a critical study, *Museum Mediations.* She teaches at The Hudson Valley Writers' Center, where she is co-editor of Slapering Hol Press, and she is a poetry editor at *Boston Review.* She lives in Sleepy Hollow, New York.

ABOUT THE ARTIST

SARAH GRIFFIN THIBODEAUX is a contemporary realist artist living in New Orleans. She paints the figure, still life, landscape, and portrait, using the alla prima technique. Thibodeaux studied at the New Orleans Academy of Fine Arts, Art Students League, and the Florence Academy of Art. She currently teaches portrait painting and still life painting at the New Orleans Academy of Fine Arts and in workshops. Her work is held in public and private collections throughout the U.S. Her web site is www.sarahgriffinthibodeaux.com.

ABOUT THE WASHINGTON PRIZE

St. Rage's Vault is the winner of the 2012 Word Works Washington Prize. B. K. Fischer's collection was selected from among 302 manuscripts submitted by American and Canadian poets.

FIRST READERS: Barbara Anderson • Stuart Bartow • Susana Case • George Drew • Peter Fernbach • Jonathan Hall • Elaine Handley • Erich Hintze • Diane Lockward • Amy MacClennan • Marilyn McCabe • Kathleen McCoy • Yvonne Murphy • Mary Sanders Shartle

SECOND READERS: Carrie Bennett • Leslie McGrath • Jay Rogoff • Barbara Ungar • Rosemary Winslow

FINAL JUDGES: Karren Alenier • Jennifer Barber • J. H. Beall • Nancy White

OTHER WASHINGTON PRIZE BOOKS

Nathalie F. Anderson, *Following Fred Astaire,* 1998
Michael Atkinson, *One Hundred Children Waiting for a Train,* 2001
Carrie Bennett, *biography of water*, 2004
Peter Blair, *Last Heat*, 1999
Richard Carr, *Ace*, 2008
Ann Rae Jonas, *A Diamond Is Hard But Not Tough*, 1997
Frannie Lindsay, *Mayweed*, 2009
Richard Lyons, *Fleur Carnivore*, 2005
Fred Marchant, *Tipping Point*, 1993, 3rd printing 1999
Ron Mohring, *Survivable World*, 2003
Brad Richard, *Motion Studies*, 2010
Jay Rogoff, *The Cutoff*, 1994
Prartho Sereno, *Call from Paris*, 2007
Enid Shomer, *Stalking the Florida Panther*, 1987, 2nd printing 1993
John Surowiecki, *The Hat City after Men Stopped Wearing Hats*, 2006
Miles Waggener, *Phoenix Suites*, 2002
Mike White, *How to Make a Bird with Two Hands*, 2011
Nancy White, *Sun, Moon, Salt*, 1992, 2nd edition 2010

ABOUT THE WORD WORKS

The Word Works, a nonprofit literary organization, publishes contemporary poetry and presents public programs. Since 1981, it has sponsored the Washington prize, a monetary award to and book publication for an American or Canadian poet. Monthly, The Word Works offers free literary programs in the Chevy Chase, MD, Café Muse series, and each summer, it holds free poetry programs in Washington, DC's Rock Creek Park. Annually in June, two high school students debut in the Miller Poetry Series as winners of the Jacklyn Potter Young Poets Competition.

Since 1974, Word Works programs have included: "In the Shadow of the Capitol," a symposium and archival project on the African American intellectual community in segregated Washington, DC; the Gunston Arts Center Poetry Series (e.g. Ai, Carolyn Forché, and Stanley Kunitz); the Poet Editor panel discussions at The Writer's Center (e.g. John Hollander, Maurice English, Anthony Hecht, Josephine Jacobsen); and Master Class workshops (e.g. Agha Shahid Ali, Thomas Lux, Marilyn Nelson).

As a 501(c)3 organization, The Word Works has received awards from the National Endowment for the Arts, National Endowment for the Humanities, DC Commission on the Arts & Humanities, Witter Bynner Foundation, Poets & Writers, The Writer's Center, Bell Atlantic, the David G. Taft Foundation, and others, including many generous private patrons. The Word Works has established an archive of artistic and administrative materials in the Washington Writing archive housed in the George Washington University Gelman Library. The Word Works is a member of the Council of Literary Magazines and Presses and distributed by Small Press Distribution.

More information at WordWorksBooks.org

OTHER AVAILABLE WORD WORKS BOOKS

FROM THE HILARY THAM CAPITAL COLLECTION

Mel Belin, *Flesh That Was Chrysalis*
Doris Brody, *Judging the Distance*
Sarah Browning, *Whiskey in the Garden of Eden*
Grace Cavalieri, *Pine Crest Rest Home*
Christopher Conlon, *Gilbert and Garbo in Love*
    Mary Falls: Requiem for Mrs. Surratt
Donna Denizé, *Broken Like Job*
W. Perry Epes, *Nothing Happened*
Bernadette Geyer, *The Scabbard of Her Throat*
James Hopkins, *Eight Pale Women*
Brandon Johnson, *Love's Skin*
Marilyn McCabe, *Perpetual Motion*
Judith McCombs, *The Habit of Fire*
Miles David Moore, *The Bears of Paris*
    Rollercoaster
Kathi Morrison-Taylor, *By the Nest*
Maria Terrone, *The Bodies We Were Loaned*
Hilary Tham, *Bad Names for Women*
    Counting
Barbara Ungar, *Charlotte Brontë, You Ruined My Life*
Jonathan Vaile, *Blue Cowboy*
Rosemary Winslow, *Green Bodies*
Michele Wolf, *Immersion*

INTERNATIONAL EDITIONS

Yoko Danno & James C. Hopkins, *The Blue Door*
Moshe Dor, Barbara Goldberg, Giora Leshem, eds.,
    The Stones Remember
Moshe Dor (Barbara Goldberg, trans.), *Scorched by the Sun*

Myong-Hee Kim, *Crow's Eye View: The Infamy of Lee Sang, Korean Poet*

Vladimir Levchev, *Black Book of the Endangered Species*

ADDITIONAL TITLES

Karren L. Alenier, *Wandering on the Outside*

Karren L. Alenier, Hilary Tham, Miles David Moore, eds., *Winners: A Retrospective of the Washington Prize*

Christopher Bursk, ed., *Cool Fire*

Barbara Goldberg, *Berta Broadfoot and Pepin the Short*

Jacklyn Potter, Dwaine Rieves, Gary Stein, eds., *Cabin Fever: Poets at Joaquin Miller's Cabin*

Robert Sargent, *Aspects of a Southern Story*
  A Woman From Memphis

www.ingramcontent.com/pod-product-compliance
Lightning Source LLC
Chambersburg PA
CBHW031208090426
42736CB00009B/831